ZEBULON PIKE

Lost in the Rockies

Patricia Calvert

BENCHMARK BOOKS

MARSHALL CAVENDISH
NEW YORK

For Katie and Chris Luhmann, who are explorers, too.

Benchmark Books
99 White Plains Road
Tarrytown, NY 10591-9001
www.marshallcavendish.com

All Internet sites were available and accurate when sent to press.

Library of Congress Cataloging-in-Publication Data

Calvert, Patricia.
Zebulon Pike : lost in the Rockies / by Patricia Calvert.
p. cm.—(Great explorations)
Summary: Presents the life and career of the army officer and explorer who discovered, among other
places in the West and Southwest, the great Rocky Mountain peak in Colorado that bears his name.
Includes bibliographical references and index.
ISBN 0-7614-1612-9
1. Pike, Zebulon Montgomery, 1779-1813—Juvenile literature. 2. Explorers—West (U.S.)—
Biography—Juvenile literature. 3. West (U.S.)—Discovery and exploration—Juvenile literature.
4. Southwest, New—Discovery and exploration—Juvenile literature. 5. Rocky Mountains—Discovery and
exploration—Juvenile literature. 6. West (U.S.)—Biography—Juvenile literature. [1. Pike, Zebulon Montgomery,
1779-1813. 2. Explorers. 3. Southwest, New—Discovery and exploration.
4. West (U.S.)—Discovery and exploration.] I. Title. II. Series.

F592.P653C35 2003
978'.02'092—dc22

2003017583

Photo research by Candlepants Incorporated

Cover photo: Geoffrey Clements/Corbis
Cover inset: Independence National Historical Park, by Charles Willson Peale, (c.1808)

The photographs in this book are used by permission and through the courtesy of: *North Wind Picture Archive*: 8,
9, 22, 25, 27, 31, 36, 37, 76; *Independence National Historical Park*: Charles Willson Peale (c.1796-1797), 11; James
Sharples Senior (1796), 15; Charles Willson Peale (c.1819), 59. *Corbis*; Bettmann, 20, Minnesota Historical Society,
28; 49; 73; Academy of Natural Science, Philadelphia, 51, 56; Burstein Collection, 53; Geoffrey Clements, 58;
Christie's Images, 61; Francis G. Mayer, 65. *Culver Pictures*: 34. *Amon Carter Museum, Fort Worth Texas,
Acquisition in memory of Mitchell A. Wilder, Director Amon Carter Museum, 1961-1979*: 39. *The Filson Historical
Society, Louisville, KY*: 42. *Nebraska State Historical Society*: 46. *Library of Congress*: (#LCUSZ62-50630) 68.
American Philosophical Society Library: 72. *US Army Center for Military History*: 81.
National Archives of Canada: #C-029351, 83, Stretton Sempronius/C-014905, 84.

Printed in China
1 3 5 6 4 2

Contents

foreword

Names such as Daniel Boone, Meriwether Lewis, and Kit Carson—to mention only three—come quickly to our minds when we think of the men who explored the American West and paved the way for its settlement.

The name James B. Wilkinson doesn't leap out at us, yet he played an important and rascally role in the way the West developed as it did. Born in Philadelphia in 1757, Wilkinson had intended to become a physician, but from an early age he demonstrated an appetite for adventure. He joined the Revolutionary Army and earned the rank of captain in 1775, when he was only eighteen years old.

It wasn't long before young Wilkinson demonstrated a skill for trying to bend the law to suit his own ends—including joining others in a bold plot to unseat George Washington as head of the army. Washington Irving, famous author of *The Legend of Sleepy Hollow*, said that Wilkinson would have made "an admirable trumpeter" or traveling salesman.

Others were less kind: historian Donald Jackson called Wilkinson "a knave," whose decades in public office ranged "from petty chicanery [trickery] to treason."

Two of Wilkinson's most elaborate plots involved first an invasion of Mexico and then setting up a nation of his own to be called the Mississippi Valley Confederation. He probably never guessed that a boy he met in 1793 at Fort Washington along the Ohio River would one day play an important role in those schemes. The lad, the son of the fort's commander—only fourteen years old, slender, blue eyed and brown haired—was named Zebulon Montgomery Pike.

ONE

A Slave to No Man

No officer could be more attentive, prompt and efficient . . . nor was there any more emulous [eager to excel]. . . .
—Description of Zebulon Montgomery Pike by a fellow officer

Zebulon Montgomery Pike's forebears paved the way for his own pursuit of adventure. The Pikes, whose family name appears by 1200 in the history of London, were early immigrants to the New World. By 1635 they had settled in Ipswich, Massachusetts, only seven years after the Bay Colony was founded. The men of the family became ministers, merchants, lawyers, and judges, and one of them—Robert Pike—was remarkable because he refused to impart the death sentence to those accused of witchcraft.

Zebulon Pike, the explorer's father, was born in what is today known as New Jersey and was an orphan by the age of ten. When his grandfather sent him to learn the saddle maker's trade, the boy ran off to sea. He returned shortly before the beginning of the American Revolution, married Isabella Brown on April 17, 1775, then enlisted in the Continental Army in 1776. By 1778 he had been promoted to the rank of captain and had fought in battles on Long Island, at White Plains, and at Monmouth before his discharge at the end of the war.

Zebulon and Isabella settled on a farm near the village of Lamberton (called Lamington in those days), in Somerset County, near present-day Trenton, New Jersey. Their first child died when it was nine days old, but Isabella noted in the family Bible, "Our second child Zebulon was born January 5 in the year 1779." The baby's middle name, Montgomery, was bestowed on the infant sometime after his birth, in honor of General Richard Montgomery, who had been killed near Quebec in 1775. As an adult, Zebulon always used his middle initial to distinguish himself from his father.

As a child, the family called him Zeb. He was joined by two brothers, James and George, and a sister, Maria. Both James and George suffered from consumption (tuberculosis), a disease that was common in the colonies and that caused George's death when he was nineteen. Zeb escaped tuberculosis and pushed himself to excel physically and mentally. Zeb's schoolmates remembered the future explorer as a "boy of slender form, very fair complexion, [and] gentle and retiring disposition." However, one of Pike's biographers, W. Eugene Hollon, noted, "the child was father to the man" because, combined with the boy's even temper, others also remembered that he was stubborn and self-willed, characteristics that would work both for and against him later in life.

His schooling—as was true for most boys of the era—was "slight in quality and short in duration," though he did receive some training in mathematics from a teacher named Mr. Wall. His mother also tutored

Zebulon Montgomery Pike. His father was also named Zebulon, so from an early age Zeb used his middle name or initial to set him apart.

him in reading and writing, skills that enabled him as an explorer to keep detailed journals, which in spite of some rather creative spelling and punctuation are still referred to by historians.

When the American Revolution came to a close in 1781, Zeb's father moved the family to Bucks County in eastern Pennsylvania, across the Delaware River from New Jersey. He returned to farming, but the family had hardly put down roots before moving again. This time they settled on a homestead along Bald Eagle Creek in western Pennsylvania, where the soil was rocky and crops did poorly.

Even with a team of oxen, it was backbreaking work carving a homestead out of the wilderness. The soil at the Pike farm along Bald Eagle Creek in Pennsylvania was especially rocky and poor, so the family soon moved on.

By 1790, when Zeb was eleven years old, his father had been lured even farther west, as were many settlers of the day, by the call of the "Beautiful River," the Ohio. Rather than take up farming again, Zebulon Sr. enlisted in the Pennsylvania militia. His previous military experience earned him a captain's commission and a salary of $35 per month. It wasn't much for a man with a growing family, but it would prove to be more reliable than farming.

The task of the militia was to protect colonists from Indian attacks. As increasing numbers of settlers poured into the Northwest Territory (the future states of Ohio, Indiana, Illinois, Michigan, Wisconsin, and part of Minnesota), Indian nations—including the Shawnee, Miami, and Delaware—increased their resistance to the encroachment of whites onto their lands. With the exception of a few men such as Zeb's father, the militia—commanded by General Arthur St. Clair—was a ragtag army that was "badly clothed, badly fed, and badly paid." It was made up mostly of untrained recruits, who were paid a meager $2.10 per month. Many of them had just been released from jail. These poorly disciplined, badly equipped soldiers were unable to prevent the slaughter of hundreds of colonists during an Indian attack at Greenville, Ohio, on November 4, 1791.

General William Butler, leader of the regiment in which Zeb's father served, was critically wounded in the attack and called Captain Pike to his side. "I cannot live; you load my pistol," he ordered, "and set me against a tree, and I will die fighting." The captain did as he was told, and Butler died where he stood. The Indians admired the general's courage and, hoping to acquire it themselves, they cut out his heart and ate it. The general's death had been swift; many of the colonists might have envied him, for they were horribly tortured before their own deaths.

The massacre caused a great outcry from the public and forced President Washington to realize that trained troops were needed to meet the challenge of Indian attacks on the frontier. On March 5, 1792, Congress

A Man of Questionable Character

Not everyone admired General James Wilkinson as much as young Zeb Pike did. General Winfield Scott, a hero of the War of 1812, remembered him as an "unprincipled imbecile." A territorial governor called him "a rascal through and through," and he was labeled a man who had "a rare faculty for getting into difficulties." One biographer, Jared Stallones, described Wilkinson as "a handsome, charming, silver-tongued schemer who . . . had a finger in every pie and whose only loyalty was to his own pocketbook."

General James Wilkinson, once a friend of General Anthony Wayne, hoped to take over the position of commander of the army of the West. He eventually did but only after Wayne's unexpected death in 1796.

Young Zeb Pike was fourteen years old when his father moved the family to Fort Washington, located on the Ohio River near present-day Cincinnati.

voted to send 5,120 trained soldiers to the West under the command of General Anthony Wayne—nicknamed Mad Anthony—a hero of the American Revolution. The same day, Zeb's father, then forty years old and responsible for a wife and four children, applied for a commission in the regular forces under Wayne's command and moved the family to Fort Washington, near what is now Cincinnati. The long-range aim of the U.S. government—in spite of the massacre at Greenville—was eventually to build a string of forts in areas where new territory was claimed.

Young Zeb was fourteen years old, James was eight, Maria was four, and George, born on April 7, 1793, was only a few weeks old when the family settled in a log house at Fort Washington. It was an exciting and dangerous time and place for a boy to come of age. Every day, Zeb witnessed the life-and-death decisions that were made by the soldiers.

"Number Thirteen"

General Wilkinson had twice been forced to resign his military commission just as his unscrupulous activities were about to come to light. In 1777 he was involved with General Thomas Conway in a plot, called the Conway Cabal, whose purpose was to discredit General George Washington as head of the Revolutionary Army and replace him with General Horatio Gates. When the plot was revealed, Wilkinson informed on Conway and Gates. It would not be the last time he betrayed co-conspirators or his character was called into question. In 1787 Wilkinson aligned himself with the Spanish governor of New Orleans, Esteban Miro, and became a double agent whom the Spanish government paid $2,000 a year to act as an informant. His code name was Number Thirteen. Wilkinson even swore allegiance to the Spanish government—which controlled what are now the states of Florida, Texas, New Mexico, and California—an act of treason that was punishable by death.

Zeb—who was idealistic and impressionable—especially admired General James Wilkinson, a dashing, flamboyant officer, often dressed in a two-toned blue uniform decorated with gold braid. He seemed to exude an air of courage and daring. Wilkinson, twenty-two years older than Zeb, was fated to play a defining role in the boy's life, though neither of them could have guessed it in 1793. Given Zeb's admiration for the flashy young general, as well as for his father and General Wayne, it came as no surprise when, at the age of fifteen, he enlisted in the army, too. For him, a career in the military was as natural as breathing the air of the frontier.

Later in life, Zeb vowed, "You will either hear of my fame or my death," but early on there was little to indicate that he was much different from other adolescents his age. He was of medium height—five feet eight—and described as "tolerably square and robust." One trait set him apart, however: in an era when many young men drank to excess, Zeb abstained. Gambling and fighting were also pastimes for some—but not for young Pike. Instead he spent his spare time working to improve his mathematical skills and studying French. His detractors sometimes snickered behind his back and called him a prude, but it did not deter the young and ambitious soldier.

From the beginning of his military career, however, Zeb dreamed of distinguishing himself—to the point that he might have stretched the truth a bit along the way. He claimed to have been involved in General Wayne's victory over the Indians at the Battle of Fallen Timbers on August 20, 1794, when he was only fifteen. There is no proof that he was ever there. Instead his earliest duties as a private were in the Quartermaster Corps, which supplied food, clothing, and other essentials to the troops under his father's command. The supplies were transported by keelboat from Fort Washington to his father's new post at Fort Massac, 40 miles (64 kilometers) east of the point where the Ohio River joins the Mississippi.

When General Wayne died in 1796, James Wilkinson—despite the scandal that had twice forced him out of the army—assumed command of what was now called the western army. Earlier, Wilkinson probably

General Anthony Wayne earned the respect of his troops during the Revolutionary War, as well as the nickname Mad Anthony. In August 1794 he and his men defeated a group of Indian fighters at the Battle of Fallen Timbers.

had paid little attention to Zeb, but over the years he noted the way the twenty year old performed his duties—with a discipline and dedication that were often lacking in other enlisted men. In 1799 Wilkinson promoted him to the rank of second lieutenant. Eight months later, Zeb became a full lieutenant and so began a lifelong association between the two men.

One of Zeb's responsibilities as a lieutenant was to keep new recruits in line. In the early days of the frontier, perhaps because of harsh living conditions combined with deep boredom, "the most vexatious [troubling] evil . . . was the general and extensive use of Ardent Spirits." Zeb, who was "uniformly abstemious," had little patience with drunkards. Late one evening, as he and a fellow officer returned to the fort from a visit to Pittsburgh, they hid themselves in heavy brush to catch some soldiers suspected of carousing. They jumped out and accosted the culprits, who later were vigorously punished.

Aside from training recruits, Zeb's promotions did not mean an expansion of his duties. He continued to ship supplies to forts down the Ohio River. On the way, he often stopped to visit his wealthy uncle's plantation at Sugar Grove, Kentucky, about 15 miles (24 kilometers) from Cincinnati. The young man's rank—and perhaps the fact that he was considered "tolerably handsome"—might have charmed his eighteen-year-old cousin Clarissa Brown, whom Zeb soon fondly called Clara. She was a tall, serious-minded girl who always dressed in black and seemed older than her years. She was better educated than most girls of her day, and Zeb was duly impressed when he discovered that she wrote and spoke fluent French.

When Zeb asked for her hand in marriage, however, her father, Captain James Brown, refused to give the couple his blessing. He believed the young man had few prospects and wouldn't be able to properly support his daughter, who was accustomed to many privileges. In 1801, as young lovers everywhere have often done, Zeb and Clara ran off to

Cincinnati and were married anyway. As a wedding gift, Zeb presented his bride with one of his most treasured possessions, a book of philosophy entitled *The Economy of Human Life*, by Robert Dodsley. She kept it by her side until her death; it was lost in 1890 in a fire that destroyed most of the family's possessions.

The marriage caused a deep rift between the two families, and never again was Zeb Pike welcome in his uncle's home. Even his own father chastised Zeb for his behavior, causing the young man to admit that "youth is subject to errors and wants the cool and correct judgment" of its elders. Nevertheless he didn't hesitate to justify his actions. "Whilst I have . . . breath I will never be the slave of any man," he declared. The remark summed up Zebulon Montgomery Pike's sentiments regarding his father-in-law and expressed a philosophy that he believed would guide him honorably through life. Whether it did or not is something students of history continue to discuss.

TWO

All Strangers Are Enemies

[P]roceed up the Mississippi with all possible diligence . . . noting rivers, creeks, Highlands, Prairies, Islands, rapids, shoals, mines, Quarries, Timber, water, soil, Indian Villages and Settlements, in a diary.
—Letter to Zebulon Pike, July 30, 1805, from James Wilkinson

The newlyweds began married life at Fort Knox, along the Wabash River, near the present city of Vincennes, Indiana. The outpost, which had once been a French fort, was manned by about a hundred troops and lacked any charm. An observer went so far as to call it a "a mean looking village," whose "low banks were covered with weeds rotten from the floods. . . . The air stank." As if that weren't bad enough, "The French residents were lazy, bad-tempered outlaws. . . . Most of the first

Americans to move there were also riffraff." Clara Pike found life at this crude fort difficult, and her husband reported to his family that she felt lonesome and low spirited.

In 1803 Zeb was transferred to Fort Kaskaskia along the Mississippi, 50 miles (80 kilometers) south of Saint Louis. Living conditions for the eighty families residing there weren't much better than in Indiana. "Nothing is to be seen but houses in ruins and abandoned because the French . . . have become the laziest and most ignorant of men . . . clothed in the manner of savages."

Among those who briefly visited Kaskaskia was a red-haired, twenty-nine-year-old lieutenant named Meriwether Lewis. In April 1803, President Thomas Jefferson had completed the Louisiana Purchase for $15 million, doubling the size of the new American nation. In March 1804, almost a year after the treaty was signed, Congress divided the huge territory into two separate parcels to make its administration easier. The area south of the thirty-third parallel, which included the important seaport of New Orleans at the mouth of the Mississippi River, was called Lower Louisiana. The larger part north of the parallel, called Upper Louisiana, later became the states of Arkansas, Missouri, Iowa, Nebraska, and parts of Oklahoma, Kansas, Minnesota, North and South Dakota, Colorado, Wyoming, and Montana.

Lewis, who had been Jefferson's aide-de-camp, was recruiting men to join him and Captain William Clark on an expedition to the lands west of the Mississippi. It was a chance for the type of adventure that Zeb, only a few years younger than his visitor, had always dreamed of. Lewis made it clear, however, that he was recruiting only soldiers, not officers.

In any case, Clara was suffering from fever (probably malaria), and the children had been ill. Zeb couldn't have left the fort anyway since he wasn't merely an officer, he was its commander. On May 14, 1804, Lewis and Clark left Camp Wood, near Saint Louis, and headed up the Missouri River with a party of thirty-one men and Lewis's Newfoundland

In 1803 Pike was given the command of Fort Kaskaskia, south of Saint Louis. Among his visitors was red-haired Meriwether Lewis, who was recruiting men for the explorer's famed expedition with William Clark.

dog, Seaman. The journey of the Corps of Discovery, as Jefferson called the expedition, was destined to become the most illustrious chapter of exploration in American history.

In 1805, a year after Lewis and Clark's departure, twenty-six-year-old Zeb Pike unexpectedly got a chance for the kind of adventure he craved. He received a letter from General Wilkinson, who had recently been made governor of Upper Louisiana, asking him to come at once to Saint Louis. From there, Wilkinson intended to send Zeb north into

THE PASSAGE WEST

The boundaries of the Louisiana Purchase weren't clearly defined in the agreement signed in Paris in April 1803. France had obtained the territory three years earlier from Spain, then sold it to the United States, primarily because Napoléon needed money for his military campaigns. Little was known about the land west of the Mississippi, but Thomas Jefferson as well as many other people of the time believed it might be possible to use various waterways—the Missouri River in particular—to get all the way to the Pacific coast. One of Jefferson's main instructions to Lewis and Clark before they set out on their expedition was to look for this so-called Northwest Passage.

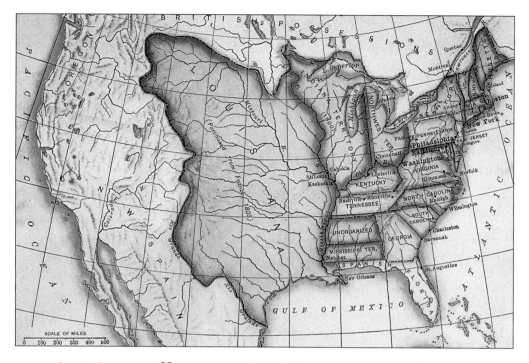

President Thomas Jefferson completed the Louisiana Purchase in April 1803. As a result, the young nation gained 830,000 square miles (2,150,000 square kilometers) of new territory.

present-day Minnesota to investigate whether Leech Lake was in fact the source of the Mississippi River.

However, the area didn't really need to be explored, not in the same sense that Lewis and Clark needed to explore the unknown territory west of the Mississippi. During the previous one hundred years it had been thoroughly surveyed by British, French, and American fur traders. Trading posts had been built, and alliances with the Indian tribes had been forged, especially by the British and French. Pike was warned not to create trouble among the Indians that he met, but to take careful note of appropriate sites for future forts and trading posts.

The Lewis and Clark expedition received a great deal of coverage in the press of the day, but Wilkinson had dispatched Pike upriver in secret, without President Jefferson's knowledge. Fortunately when Jefferson was later informed of the venture, he indicated his approval.

On Friday afternoon, August 9, 1805, five months before his twenty-seventh birthday, Zeb Pike set out from Fort Bellefontaine, a few miles

A Whiff of Scandal

General Wilkinson's orders to Zeb Pike were to "ascend the main branches of the River, until you reach the source of it . . . before the waters are froze up." Pike didn't leave until August 9, 1805, however, making it unlikely that he could fulfill such orders before the winter freeze. Wilkinson clearly had other motives. He had established a secret partnership with wealthy Saint Louis fur trader René Auguste Chouteau and his son Pierre. As governor he intended to use his power and influence to help the Saint Louis traders establish a monopoly in the fur trade in the northern areas that now belonged to the United States and would become present-day Wisconsin and Minnesota.

How much did Pike know about his mentor's plans? Later, Pike's critics said that he "knew what he was to do . . . and did it"— in other words, his real mission was to learn as much about the French and British fur trade as possible, a task best performed in the wintertime at the height of the fur-trapping season. Pike was quick to defend both his mentor and himself, though, and claimed that the idea for the expedition had in fact originated with Meriwether Lewis, not Wilkinson.

upriver from Saint Louis. He took with him a crew of twenty men: seventeen privates, two corporals, and a sergeant. A 70-foot (21-meter) keelboat was loaded with $2,000 worth of supplies—"flour, cornmeal, pork, gunpowder, salt . . . tents, clothing, blankets"—enough, he hoped, to last four months. Also on board were whiskey, tobacco, hunting knives, and bolts of bright cotton cloth to be used in trading with the Indians. But no one aboard spoke any of the dialects of the Indian tribes that the expedition was likely to encounter. Nor was there a doctor among the crew.

Fresh meat—an important item, because each man would most likely consume between 7 and 8 pounds (3.2 and 3.6 kilograms) per day—didn't travel well, but could be regularly obtained by hunting deer, elk, or bison along the way. Smaller game such as rabbits, opossums, ducks, and turkeys was also plentiful. Until the river froze, there would be an ample supply of fish as well.

In Pike's time, the Mississippi River north of Saint Louis was shallow and wide—5 to 6 miles (8 to 9.7 kilometers) from bank to bank—and dotted with hundreds of small islands. In times of flood, it was impossible to tell where the main channel was, making it easy to run aground on a sandbar. Yet early in the journey, because of strong winds from the south that filled the keelboat's single square canvas sail, the expedition sometimes covered 40 miles (64 kilometers) per day.

Heading north, of course, meant going against the current. If winds weren't favorable, the keelboat had to be rowed or poled upstream or towed with ropes by men who walked along the riverbank, which was densely overgrown with thickets of cottonwoods, ash, and hackberries. Despite the early progress, the Mississippi quickly proved to be more of an adversary than a friend. On August 16, Zeb noted in his journal, "[we] were so unfortunate as to get fast on a log; and did not extricate ourselves until past eleven o'clock, having to saw off [the] log under the water."

Things got worse. Three days later, "our boat struck a sawyer" (another submerged log) and soon began to take on water through the hole that had been punched in its side. The crew got the boat to a strip of beach, where "we with great difficulty keeled [overturned] her . . . cut out the plank and put in a new one." Food, clothing, and equipment were soaked, and the rest of the day was spent drying everything in the sun.

Four days later, on August 20, near what is now Keokuk, Iowa, the keelboat came to an 11-mile (18-kilometer) stretch of rapids, "with several successive ridges and shoals. . . . The first has the greatest fall and is the most difficult to ascend." In order to traverse the rapids safely, William Ewing, a U.S. government agent who dealt with the Sauk Indians, suggested that Zeb take aboard some of the river-savvy young Sauks who were traveling in his own party and who knew how to navigate the rapids safely.

The following day, Zeb made his first speech to the Indians. In it he served notice that the Americans had arrived in the north country and

Pike and his men crossed the lands of several Indian nations on their journey. Some were friendly. Others, such as the Sioux, resented the intrusion of white trappers, traders, and explorers in their territory.

were a force to be reckoned with. He presented tobacco, knives, and whiskey to the Indians as tokens of friendship and noted in his journal that he was pleased when the Indians "thanked me for the good opinion I had of their nation . . . [and] were glad to see me among them." To conserve his supply of whiskey, Pike later gave the Indians only "made" whiskey, or a three-to-one mixture of water and liquor.

Zeb—an experienced hunter since boyhood—had brought two of his favorite hunting dogs with him, as well as his personal rifle, a far better weapon than those issued by the army. On August 24, 1805, he and Corporal Samuel Bradley took the dogs and went ashore to get fresh meat. The dogs vanished in the high grass, and as Pike and Bradley searched for them they discovered evidence that Indians had recently passed through the area.

It was an unnerving moment, so Pike and Bradley retreated to the boat. Later two of the crew went ashore to search again for the dogs. This time it was the men who disappeared. Zeb had made it clear that the "boat never waited for any person on shore" so, after firing several shots to let the absent soldiers know he was leaving, Zeb departed without either the missing men or his dogs on board. He continued to fire off a shot every hour, but no answering shots were heard.

Four days later, Zeb's apprehension increased when five dead dogs were seen hanging from a pole onshore. His own dogs, whose fate was never determined, did not seem to be among the five. Nevertheless it was a harsh reminder that he was in a foreign land still dominated by Indian nations whose customs were often hard to fathom. As Pike later noted in his journal, he had entered a region where "all strangers are enemies."

Although the weather was still summerlike back at Fort Bellefontaine, late in the month a cold north wind whipped in, and the temperature dropped to 10 degrees Fahrenheit. Zeb suffered a severe bout of fever and dysentery, yet on Sunday, September 1, 1805, he forced himself to go ashore at a settlement at Dubuque, Iowa, named in 1788 for its French-

Canadian founder, Julien Dubuque. Pike's spirits were lifted when he was told that the two men who had gone ashore near Keokuk were still alive. They had been "six days without anything to eat except muscles [mussels, or river clams]," when they were found wandering in the woods by James Aird, a Scottish representative of the Michilimackinac Trading Company. Aird's "humanity and attention" had saved their lives.

The countryside near present-day La Crosse, Wisconsin, was known for its striking and steep bluffs. French traders named the settlement after the shape of the racket Indians used in one of their games. It suggested a bishop's cross.

On September 10, when a break came in the cold rain, the crew shot pigeons for supper. The expedition continued up the Mississippi as if it were climbing the rungs of a ladder, passing Prairie du Chien, Wisconsin, a former French settlement above the mouth of the Wisconsin River. There, Pike hired two interpreters, Pierre Rousseau and Joseph Renville, who were paid twenty-five cents per day for their services. Next they passed present-day La Crosse, then headed on to La Crescent, Minnesota. By September 21, the explorers reached the site of the future capital of Minnesota, Saint Paul.

One of Pike's outstanding accomplishments occurred two days later, on September 23, near the spot where, in 1820, Fort Snelling would be

On September 15, 1805, Pike paid the Sioux $200 for 150,000 acres (60,702 hectares) overlooking the Mississippi River. Fifteen years later, Fort Snelling was built on the site, where it still stands today.

built on "the finest site on the Mississippi river." The lieutenant negotiated a treaty with the local Sioux Indians to purchase 150,000 acres (60,702 hectares) of land in exchange for $200 worth of trade goods. Ironically Wilkinson—who spent lavishly on himself—grumbled about the sum, complaining that Pike was "a much better soldier than negotiator."

Pike kept his men heading north, as winter descended with freezing swiftness. By October 3, 1805, with the mercury at 0 degrees Fahrenheit, the hunters bagged "three geese, and one raccoon; also a *brilau* [a badger], an animal which I never saw before." On October 16, the men woke to discover it had snowed in the night. Nevertheless Pike was determined to get as far upriver as possible, eager to perform the tasks he'd been given by Wilkinson. But by this time his men were severely exhausted, ill, and numbed by cold. Pike realized he had no choice but to put the boat ashore and give the crew a few days to rest and recuperate.

Once onshore, Sergeant Kennerman, "one of the stoutest men I ever knew, broke a blood vessel and vomited nearly two quarts of blood," Zeb wrote. Corporal Bradley, who'd earlier gone hunting with Pike, passed "a pint of blood when he attempted to void his urine." Pike was forced to acknowledge that "these unhappy circumstances, in addition to the [illness] of four other men," meant the journey had to be halted indefinitely so a permanent camp could be made.

T H R E E

Winter in the North Country

*I began to conceive the life of a Hunter to be a very slavish [lowly]
one . . . which I was obliged to do to keep my men from starving.*
—Entry in Pike's journal, November 16, 1805

In mid-October near the Swan River in northern Minnesota, near present-day Little Falls, Pike estimated that he was about 1,500 miles (2,415 kilometers) from Saint Louis. His men badly needed a rest, as did he. The area was rich with game and stands of tall pines, and on October 18 Pike set "every hand to work" to build another permanent camp.

Sixty logs were cut, trimmed, and set in place for a 36-square-foot (3.3-square-meter) stockade anchored by a pair of blockhouses from which the fort could be defended in the event of an Indian attack. While the other men labored, Pike, John Sparks, and Samuel Bradley,

Hunters in the early West were especially fond of bear meat because it was so rich in fat. It provided more energy to weary trappers and explorers than deer or elk meat, which tended to be leaner.

the ablest hunters in the group, made sure that everyone was well fed, on one day killing four bears and a deer weighing 137 pounds (62 kilograms). Bear meat was prized because its high fat content provided more energy than other meats.

Large supplies of fresh meat couldn't be eaten quickly, though, so portions were either salted or smoked to preserve them. The preparation of one of the soldiers' favorite meals was simple: meat (fresh, salted, or smoked) was boiled in a pot of water along with rice or dried corn, then flour was added to thicken the stew. If meat was scarce, each man received only 2 pounds (0.9 kilogram) per day rather than the usual 7 to 8 pounds (3.2 to 3.6 kilograms). As a consolation, Pike sometimes added an extra ration of whiskey to the meal.

By November 7, "ice in the river [was] thickening," Pike observed, which meant fish would no longer be part of their diet. Snow began to fall heavily and soon was knee deep, making it difficult to gather wood and keep fires burning through the night for warmth. Pike complained in his journal that he was "powerfully attacked with fantastics of the brain," or delusions, brought on by a combination of severe living conditions, malnutrition, and extreme physical exhaustion.

At last, on December 10, 1805, after two canoes and two sleds had been built, Pike put Sergeant Kennerman in charge of the stockade. Then Pike and eleven others, not including Rousseau, one of the interpreters, struck out for Leech Lake, which Pike was certain would prove to be the source of the Mississippi. Each sled was loaded with supplies and hauled by two men. The canoes—more lightly loaded—were dragged across the snow by the remaining men. It was arduous work, and when the weather was bad, they covered no more than 5 miles (8 kilometers) per day.

Four days after setting out, the expedition nearly came to a halt when one of the sleds fell through the ice on the river. Pike's baggage, books, and cartridges were soaked, along with 4 pounds (1.8 kilograms) of

DREAMS AND DELUSIONS

Throughout the centuries, explorers around the world have experienced "fantastics of the brain," a malady that Pike described. Extreme physical stress—hunger, heat, cold, and illness—caused men to see visions of animals or people that weren't actually there, to hear unusual sounds, or to imagine they had already died.

At the end of Pike's own century, Admiral Robert E. Peary at the North Pole and later Ernest Shackleton at the South Pole, to name but two adventurers, eloquently described the same affliction. To fend off such mental aberrations, Pike reread the few books he'd brought along on the journey. He tended to his journal. He hunted. And always he kept at the forefront of his mind his desire to fulfill General Wilkinson's instructions: find the headwaters of the Mississippi.

powerful Sussex gunpowder. The baggage and books could be dried out, but the gunpowder and some of the cartridges were a loss. The sled itself was too badly broken to be repaired, and three days were spent building a new one.

During the cold weather, wet clothing was not merely uncomfortable, it was life threatening. Water-soaked garments robbed the wearer of precious body heat and made him more vulnerable to death by freezing. At night, at makeshift camps, damp articles were dried near the fire.

While his men worked, Pike once again used the time to hunt and eventually needed help bringing back eleven deer and a buffalo. In order to have room to carry the fresh meat, it was necessary to leave some of the other supplies behind. Pike ordered his men to dig a pit 4 feet (1.2 meters) deep and 3 feet (0.9 meter) wide, in which a barrel of flour and another of salt pork were buried. Dirt was shoveled over the cache, or hiding place, a large fire was then built on the spot, allowed to die out, then the ashes were scattered about to further disguise it from the Indians.

Christmas Day, 1805, turned out to be a meager celebration: "Gave out two pound[s] [0.9 kilogram] of extra meat—2 pound[s] of extra flour, one gill [about $\frac{1}{4}$ pint, or 4 ounces, or 0.1 liter] of whiskey and some tobacco per man."

On January 4, 1806, several of the tents were damaged by fire, leaving the men even more exposed to the bitter north winds. The snow got ever deeper. Pike usually walked ahead, clearing a trail and building fires along the way so that the men would be able to warm themselves and rest. He pushed himself almost beyond the limit of endurance, admitting, "Never did I undergo more fatigue," as he performed "the duties of hunter, spy, guide, commanding officer." Creating a trail, then turning back to make sure his men were still following, meant that Pike actually covered more miles and expended even more energy than they did. "At night I was scarcely able to make my notes intelligible."

About two o'clock on the afternoon of February 1, 1806, Pike stood at last on the frozen shores of Leech Lake, 30 miles (48 kilometers) west of Grand Rapids, Minnesota. "I will not attempt to describe my feeling on the accomplishment of my voyage," he declared, elated by his discovery of the headwaters of the Mississippi River, which flows some 2,400 miles (3,864 kilometers) from its origin in Minnesota to the Gulf of Mexico. Pike erred by 25 miles (40 kilometers), however, for when he came to a fork in the river he decided to take the western branch. Later exploration revealed that the eastern branch led to Lake Itasca, the true source of the Mississippi.

Soon after his arrival at Leech Lake, a welcome treat awaited Pike and his men at the nearby headquarters of the British Northwest Company, an outpost of civilization in the frozen wilderness. They were greeted by the company's manager, Hugh McGillis, and given strong, hot coffee, bread, butter, and cheese. Later McGillis provided Pike with two sled dogs worth $200 for his journey back to Saint Louis. Pike was amazed that the Englishman also had a fine library and was surprised

One of the reasons General Wilkinson sent Pike upriver was to assess the potential of the fur trade in the North. Furs were a valuable commodity over which French, British, and American trappers competed.

that settlers in the region lived so well. "They have horses, raise plenty of Irish potatoes, catch pike, suckers, and pickerel, and white fish in abundance."

Yet in spite of his host's considerable hospitality, Pike informed McGillis that the Englishman could no longer fly the British flag in what—after the Louisiana Purchase—had become American territory. To make sure that his point was clearly understood, Pike ordered his men to shoot down the Union Jack while McGillis watched—speechless, no doubt!—then hoisted the American flag in its place.

General Wilkinson had been especially interested in establishing friendly relations with the various Indian groups and had instructed Pike to escort several chiefs back to Saint Louis for a personal meeting.

Indians had long trapped furs for their own use. After the arrival of foreign traders, they exchanged the furs for guns and gunpowder as well as for coffee, tea, sugar, and other goods.

McGillis—in spite of the flag incident—offered to help Pike achieve that goal by inviting several chiefs to a council.

When the chiefs were asked to accompany the American visitor back to Saint Louis, however, all of them declined. Pike chided them, whereupon two young men—not the tribal chiefs that Wilkinson had requested—reluctantly agreed to make the trip. Pike rewarded each man with a blanket, leggings, a pair of scissors, a looking glass, and a portion of whiskey.

The return to Saint Louis began February 18, 1806. Within ten days, the two Indians deserted, taking their gifts with them. A week later, Pike realized he was exhausted to the point of collapse. His feet were bleeding from repeated frostbite; his ankles were swollen to twice their normal size. He looked forward with a touch of desperation to reaching the Swan River camp and the stored food he had left hidden there.

An unpleasant surprise awaited him, though, when he arrived at the camp on March 5. Pike discovered that Sergeant Kennerman, whom he had regarded so highly, had pillaged all the food and had drunk the whiskey or else sold it to the Indians. Kennerman was so bold he'd even rifled Pike's trunk and passed out his personal belongings. Perhaps because he'd once been so fond of the sergeant, Pike merely demoted Kennerman to the rank of private. Any other commander probably would have ordered him shot.

Pike, too discouraged to go on, stayed at the small fort for several days, regaining his strength. By March 18, after the river ice had melted and canoe travel was possible, Pike and his men headed downstream. Near the Spunk River, they found themselves at the lodge of a Menominee chief. The chief welcomed the Americans kindly and gave them hot food and dry clothes. He also offered to share one of his several wives with Pike.

Pike replied that he had but one wife and "considered it strictly my duty to remain faithful to her." The chief thought it was a strange custom and pointed out that he knew of many white traders who kept

A Game of Lacrosse

Whereas the journey upstream had taken several months, the voyage back to Saint Louis took a little more than three weeks. So the party decided to make a three-day stop at Prairie du Chien, Wisconsin. While there, Pike and his men were entertained by a ball game the Indians played. Contestants carried nets on the end of 3-foot (0.9-meter) sticks and sought to drive a small, hard, leather-covered ball between an opponent's goalposts set about half a mile (0.8 kilometer) apart. The game, which lasted several hours, involved passing, kicking, or knocking the ball from player to player. The Sioux were better at throwing the ball and won the game, but Pike observed that their Fox and Winnebago opponents were better runners.

Pike and his men were surprised to discover the many games of sport enjoyed by various Indian nations. When the waters of the Mississippi River froze, the Sioux played a game similar to hockey.

several wives. "All our great men each had one wife," Pike insisted. The chief nodded and smiled, but said he preferred "to have as many wives as he pleased."

On April 30, 1806, eight months and twenty-one days after their departure, the explorers were back home, having expected to be gone only four months. In their almost nine-month expedition, they had covered 5,000 miles (8,050 kilometers), and Zeb had faithfully kept the diary that Wilkinson had requested. But if Pike believed his successful return would bring him a measure of fame, it was not to be. One historian of western exploration, Robert E. Riegel, went so far as to declare Pike's accomplishments disappointingly meager. Others pointed out the deficiencies of his journey:

- *He had been charged with locating the headwaters of the Mississippi; he missed the river's origin by 25 miles (40 kilometers).*
- *Wilkinson had specifically requested that Indian chiefs from each of the northern nations be escorted to Saint Louis for face-to-face talks; none came.*
- *Pike hadn't located any streams, rivers, or lakes whose existence hadn't been already recorded—and named—by others.*
- *The British were to be convinced they could no longer trade with the Indians without paying tariffs to the United States; for years, they continued to trade as they wished.*

Pike had also hoped for an immediate promotion, along with an extended vacation during which he could recover his health and spend time with his family. He got neither. Instead, Wilkinson had another assignment for him and made it clear that it was to commence as soon as possible.

f O U R

Across the Vast Plains

[Y]ou are herewith furnished six hundred Dollars. . . . Wishing you
a safe and successfull [sic] expedition. . . .
—Letter to Zebulon Pike from James Wilkinson, June 24, 1806

As they endured the freezing temperatures of the Minnesota north country, Zebulon Pike didn't hesitate to ask himself and his men to give everything they could to accomplish their mission. Back in Saint Louis, however, General Wilkinson had been busy hatching new schemes.

One of the general's schemes had begun even before Pike was sent to find the headwaters of the Mississippi. In June 1805, two months before Pike left Bellefontaine, Wilkinson arranged to meet secretly with an old friend, Aaron Burr. (How revealing that many of Wilkinson's meetings took place in secret.) Years before, Wilkinson and Burr had

General James B. Wilkinson enjoyed fine clothes, including specially made uniforms. Many of his schemes were hatched in order to support and further his grand lifestyle.

conspired with General Thomas Conway and several others in a plot to oust George Washington as head of the Revolutionary Army and replace him with General Horatio Gates. Almost thirty years later, on July 11, 1804, Burr, then vice president of the United States, killed Alexander Hamilton, the former secretary of state, in a duel. Burr expected to be acquitted of the charge of murder—and was—but his reputation in the East was shattered. Burr looked to the West for his future—and to the powerful influence of General Wilkinson.

The two men engaged in a four-day conference at Fort Massac on the Ohio River. Wilkinson and Burr—each as greedy and ambitious as the other—discussed the possibility of equipping a private army, then invading Mexico to free it from Spanish rule. Their primary goal had nothing to do with freedom, however.

Spain prohibited free trade with the United States, but if Mexico were liberated, the two men imagined they could reap huge profits from the commerce that would open up as a result. Wilkinson and Burr had another grand dream, that Kentucky, Tennessee, Ohio, and part of Georgia and the Carolinas be encouraged to secede from the Union and become part of a new Mississippi Valley republic under their control.

Wilkinson realized that before he and Burr could take action in the Southwest they needed to know much more about Spanish activities in the area that would eventually became the states of Texas, New Mexico, Arizona, Utah, Colorado, Nevada, and California. Because the Louisiana Purchase had been transacted without making clear the borders between Spanish and American holdings, President Jefferson believed the southwestern border of the purchase was the Rio Grande. The Spanish took it to be the Arroyo Hondo, a steep-sided gulch near the Red River between the Sabine River and the town of Natchitoches. (The Red River forms the border between present-day Oklahoma and Texas.) The United States agreed to set the border at the Sabine River, which left the area between the river and the Arroyo Hondo a sort of no-man's-land of unclaimed territory. In 1805 Spain sent soldiers west of the Sabine River as American soldiers braced themselves at Fort Claiborne, east of the Arroyo Hondo.

Tensions between the two nations increased. It seemed that war was inevitable and that this climate of uncertainty perfectly suited the aims of Wilkinson and Burr. What they needed now was a spy, a man who could be trusted to be discreet. Wilkinson was sure he knew of just such a person: Zebulon Montgomery Pike.

After returning from his mission in the North, Zeb Pike wanted nothing more than to rest and to prepare his journal for publication, for he believed his reputation and future fame rested on it. In the back of Zeb's mind echoed the words of praise that newspapers had heaped on each dispatch that President Jefferson had received from Lewis and Clark. More than anything, Pike yearned to be as admired as they were.

But a time of rest, reflection, and the plotting of his future fame were not to be. The orders that Wilkinson officially handed to Pike on June 24, 1806, less than two months after his homecoming, instructed Pike to prepare for a journey to the Rocky Mountains. They contained several parts:

- *Pike's first mission was to return fifty-one Osage warriors and their families (who had been captured by the Potawatomi nation, then turned over to the United States) to their homes along the Osage River.*
- *Next he was to negotiate peace between the Osage and their traditional enemies, the Kansas Indians.*
- *When that had been accomplished, he was to travel into the territory dominated by the Pawnee and Comanche, two of the most warlike groups on the plains, and establish friendly relations.*
- *He was then to explore the Osage River (a tributary of the Missouri), identify the source of the Arkansas River, and finally explore the Red River.*

Wilkinson was well aware, however, that the river exploration would take Pike dangerously close to the territory of New Mexico, still controlled by Spain. It was important not to rile the Spanish. Therefore he cautioned Pike, "it will be necessary that you should move with great circumspect, to keep clear of any hunting or reconnoitering parties from [New Mexico] and to prevent alarm or offense." Wilkinson also hinted that if certain persons in Saint Louis learned about Pike's mission, they might alert the Spanish. That could mean the Spanish would hunt him down and take him into custody.

In his letter, the general warned that Pike would "be held responsible for [the] consequences" if the Spanish caught him in their domain, and on this subject he added, "I refer you to your orders." Were secret orders conveyed verbally to Pike, or were they written down and later destroyed? Eminent historians such as Elliot Coues believe that Pike clearly understood that his mission was to secretly explore a possible future trade route to Santa Fe should Wilkinson and Burr's plot prove successful.

By July 15, 1806, two months before Lewis and Clark returned to great public acclaim from their momentous journey to the Pacific Ocean and back, Pike and eighteen of the same men who'd gone up the Mississippi with him—including the scoundrel Kennerman—left Saint Louis and headed up the Missouri River in two keelboats. General Wilkinson's son, Lieutenant James B. Wilkinson, and an acquaintance of his, twenty-four-year-old Dr. John H. Robinson, volunteered for the journey. Also included was Antoine Vasquez, a Spanish interpreter. (If Wilkinson's plan was to avoid tangling with the Spanish, why would a Spanish interpreter be needed?)

The trip was hardly under way before Kennerman, still smarting over his demotion from sergeant to private during the previous journey, deserted the expedition. Nothing was ever heard of him again. The journey up the Mississippi the winter before had been a bitter, frostbitten experience; now traveling up the Missouri to its juncture with the Osage in the muggy heat of summer was torture of a different kind. Nor was the presence of young Wilkinson much help. Despite allowing his son to go on the expedition, the general realized the young man wasn't accustomed to hard physical labor and would need to be "tempered by degrees." Consequently he advised Pike, "Do not push him beyond his Capacities in hardship too suddenly."

As on the trip to the north country, Pike took charge of providing meat—deer, buffalo, and turkey—for his crew as well as for the Indians. Dr. Robinson accompanied him on one such hunt, when Zeb almost stepped on a rattlesnake. The doctor urged Pike to kill it and was surprised when Zeb refused. Pike, who had a reputation for being hard on men, explained that the creature had spared *his* life by not striking when it had the chance. In turn he intended to spare the snake.

From boyhood, Zebulon Pike dreamed of becoming a famed explorer.
He believed that his expedition to the Southwest would bring him the
kind of recognition that Meriwether Lewis and William Clark
enjoyed after their return from the Pacific coast.

In mid-August, the Osage were returned to their homelands at a location somewhere near the boundary between the Kansas and Missouri territories, close to the present-day city of Oswego, Kansas. A chief from the village reminded his people who it was that had returned the captives to their home. Not the Spaniards, not the French. It was "the Americans [who] stretched forth their hands," the chief pointed out.

The successful return of the prisoners meant—at least in the short term—that friendly relations prevailed between the Osage and the United States. Pike and his crew were so well received that they lingered for two weeks, during which Pike joked about all the Indian banquets that he was invited to attend. The Osage were skilled farmers and lived very well, raising "large quantities of corn, beans, and pumpkins," which they preserved by drying for use in winter.

During their stay, young Lieutenant Wilkinson displayed conduct that indicated he might share his father's selfish motives. The Osage chief, White Hair, later complained to the Indian agent in Saint Louis that the lieutenant had taken seven Osage horses without paying for them. The agent who received the information was none other than William Clark, of Lewis and Clark fame, who had been appointed to his post shortly after completing his journey to the Pacific. Clark remarked pointedly that he had gotten "very unpleasant news" about Pike's expedition.

On September 1, 1806, Pike and his men entered Pawnee territory, and the landscape became much different from anything they had seen before. Lush meadows were replaced by sandy hills barely covered with thin grass. Spanish explorers who had crossed these plains much earlier—Coronado and de Soto—also had remarked on their starkness.

"These vast plains . . . may become in time equally celebrated as the sandy desarts [sic] of Africa," Pike observed. "I saw . . . tracts of many leagues where the wind had thrown up the sand in all the fanciful form of the ocean's rolling wave, and on which not a speck of vegetable matter existed."

REMEMBERING THEIR ANCESTORS

At night the Osage camped separately from the Americans. They preferred higher ground, while the Americans stayed close to the river. Pike noted one of the Indians' habits that particularly annoyed him. "Every morning [as the sun comes up] we were awakened by the mourning of [a] savage who commenced crying . . . and continued for the space of an hour." It was the custom of the Osage to lament the loss of a relative or a friend, even if the person had been dead a long time. "Our enemies have slain my father," went one of the songs, "he is lost to me and my family; I pray to you, Oh Master of Life! to preserve me until I avenge his death." The ritual stopped as quickly as it began. Then the Indians composed themselves, went on about their tasks, only to repeat

The sandy hills might have seemed bare, but game was still plentiful, in particular large herds of *cabrie*, or pronghorn antelope. Pike estimated that on a daily basis a single hunter such as himself could easily provide fresh meat for two hundred men. On September 22, while he was hunting, Pike had an encounter with another hunter, a member of the Pawnee, a group known to be more warlike than either the Osage or the Kansas.

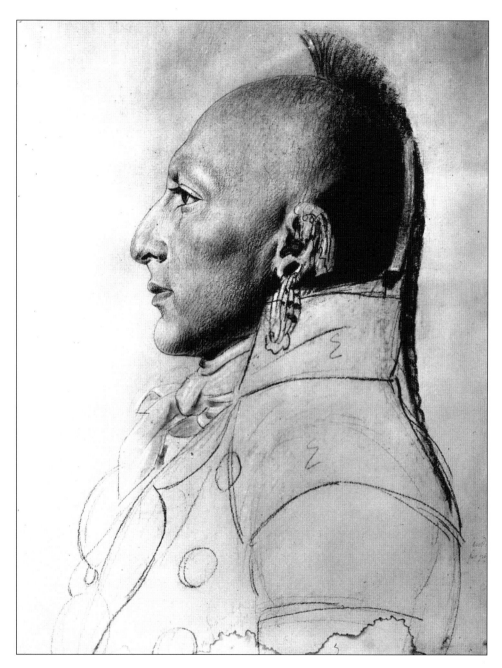

A portrait of an Osage chief, 1807. The Osage were skilled farmers who raised corn, beans, and pumpkins. Part of Pike's mission to the Southwest was to escort members of the nation back to their home near present-day Oswego, Kansas.

Pike described the Pawnee as "tall, slim [with] high cheekbones" but later criticized them as being not "so cleanly" as the Osage. Yet he admitted that when it came to "raising horses, the Pawnees are far superior to the Osage, having vast quanities of excellent horses . . . in addition [they] frequently purchase from the Spaniards."

Three days later, when Pike and his entourage entered the camp of White Wolf, the Pawnee chief, they were startled to see Spanish flags on display. White Wolf reported that six hundred Spanish dragoons, or soldiers, most of them mounted on white horses while their officers rode black ones, had recently passed through the area. Before they left, their leader, Lieutenant Facundo Melgares, had distributed gifts of Spanish flags and many medals. White Wolf reported that the dragoons were looking for Americans and had rounded up any traders they had come across and had sent them back to American territory. Pike must have suspected that the Spanish actually were on the lookout for him.

Nevertheless Pike told the Pawnee that they must give up the medals and flags because they now lived in American territory and could fly only American flags. The Pawnee reluctantly complied, but Pike could see they were troubled by something deeper than being deprived of a few mementos. After further discussion with White Wolf, it became clear that "the grand principle by which the Spaniards keep them [obedient] is fear." The Pawnee were convinced that if the Spanish came back and found American flags flying, they would attack the camp. Therefore Pike returned the Spanish flags and medals he had collected. He told White Wolf to display them to his own advantage if doing so would protect his people from the wrath of the Spaniards.

On October 1, as Pike prepared to leave the Pawnee village, White Wolf confirmed his suspicions about the Spanish presence in the region. They were searching for an expedition of Americans that might be traveling across the plains and intended to intercept it. Wilkinson's fears that certain individuals in Saint Louis might alert the Spanish to Pike's mission seemed to have come true. Or had it? Was it, in fact, Wilkinson himself who had spread the rumor? And if so, why?

The truth was that the general was in trouble again. He was about to lose his post because of repeated charges of corruption. His agreement with Burr was beginning to unravel, yet Wilkinson wanted to maintain his connection with the Spanish, still hoping he could wring some slight advantage out of it. Historians suspect that it was indeed Wilkinson himself who had alerted the Spanish to Pike's presence in the Southwest. After all, it wouldn't be the first time he had betrayed a friend. An international incident—such as leading troops into the Spanish domain to rescue Pike—would make him a hero and in the process he might be able to slice off a chunk of the territory for himself.

Herds of pronghorn antelope were a common sight on the western plains. Apart from being swift runners, antelope were also known for their curiosity, which often made them an easy target for hunters such as Pike.

GAMES ON THE GREAT

Pike observed that the Pawnee loved games as much as the Indians of the north country did. "A smooth piece of ground [was] cleared out on each side of the village for about 150 yards [137 meters]. . . . They have a large hoop of about four feet [1.2 meters] diameter in the centre of which is a small leather ring attached to leather thongs, which is extended to the hoop, and by that means keeps it in its central position; they also have a pole of about 6 feet [1.8 meters] in length, which the player holds in one hand, and then rolls the hoop from him, and immediately slides the pole after it . . . the nearer the head of the pole lies to the small ring . . . the greater the cast." The game was played by two participants at a time, but Pike admitted that he couldn't ascertain how the Indians kept score and decided when a game had been won.

White Wolf informed Pike that he had urged the Spaniards not to intrude on American territory and now he asked Pike, in turn, to respect the Spaniards' rights. In other words, he demanded that Pike halt his march across the plains. Pike brushed aside the suggestion, even when White Wolf warned him that he had already promised the Spanish he would convince the Americans to turn back.

Pike and his men were welcomed by the Pawnee during their western trek. White Wolf, a Pawnee chief, warned Pike that the Spanish were searching for Americans who had strayed illegally into the foreign territory.

On October 7, after several days of harassment on the part of Pawnee warriors and of stubborn insistence on Pike's behalf, the Americans rode peacefully out of the Pawnee camp and headed south. Pike intended to avoid a confrontation with the Spanish. On the other hand, if he could pick up their trail, it would be a good way to map the best route to Sante Fe. He reasoned that six hundred dragoons would leave an easy-to-follow trail. But within a few days, a great autumn migration of buffalo crossed the plains and nearly obliterated any trace of the route. Later heavy rains fell and wiped it out completely.

Zebulon Pike was again on his own.

FIVE

A Small Blue Cloud

We had great difficulty in getting our horses along . . . the poor ani-
mals having nearly killed themselves falling on the ice.
                    —*Zebulon Pike's journal, January 1, 1807*

On the morning of October 28, 1806, Pike sent young Lieutenant
Wilkinson down the Arkansas River with four soldiers in a pair of
canoes newly made of green cottonwood and buffalo hides. An early
snow had fallen, and on the day of his departure the general's son
wrote to his father, leaving no doubt about the conditions he faced or
his state of mind. "My men have no winter cloathing [sic], and two of
them no Blankets," he complained. "The river is now full of ice . . . last
night we had a considerable fall of Snow . . . Your Sincerely Affection-
ate tho unhappy Son."

Wilkinson packed enough supplies to last for about three weeks, but his journey actually took seventy-three days, or three and a half times as long as he had expected. Despite the challenges he faced, his was the first American expedition ever to explore what is now the state of Oklahoma.

On the same day that the general's son set off on his mission, Pike and the remaining men headed upstream to seek the source of the Arkansas River on what historian John Upton Terrell called "one of the most poorly equipped, ill-timed, injudicious, harebrained, daring ventures ever undertaken in western America."

Winter descended quickly as the expedition moved farther west. Grass, which had been sparse before, became even more scarce. "Our horses are very much jaded [starved]," Pike noted on November 8, 1806. Soon there wasn't anything for the animals to eat but the bark and withered leaves of the scattered cottonwood trees that grew along the riverbanks. One by one, as the horses "entirely gave out," they were turned loose to fend for themselves.

By mid-November, the expedition traveled out of the area that later became Kansas and drifted into what is now known as Colorado. The rolling prairie was replaced with broken, rocky terrain, making travel even more difficult. About two o'clock on the afternoon of November 15, Pike's spirits were suddenly lifted when he saw on the distant horizon "a mountain . . . which looked like a small blue cloud." He couldn't have guessed that the small blue cloud would one day bring him the fame and recognition he craved. Rather he believed he was looking at a range of mountains that were a "natural boundary between the province of Louisiana and New Mexico." The range he was facing was in fact the Rocky Mountains.

Pike led his men closer to the image he saw shimmering on the horizon, which seemed to be not that far away. (It actually was about 150 miles [242 kilometers] distant.) But the starving horses, weaker than ever, were beginning to die in their tracks. The men suffered intense misery as

DOGS OF THE PRAIRIE

Along the Arkansas River, Pike and his men took note of what they called prairie squirrels. At first glance, the animals did indeed look like short-tailed squirrels, but on the treeless expanse of the prairie they lived underground. Long before Americans crossed the plains, French traders and trappers had named these creatures *chiens*, or dogs. The animals built extensive villages—sometimes 2 square miles (5.2 square kilometers) in size—on raised stretches of ground. In an attempt to catch one of the animals alive, Pike's men poured 140 kettles of water into one of the burrows, hoping to drive the animals out. None appeared. Pike realized that the underground passages must be connected to each other and that the animals took refuge in tunnels that hadn't been flooded.

The rabbit-sized animals Pike and his men found living on the prairie reminded them of squirrels. French trappers called them chiens, or dogs, and today we call them prairie dogs.

the nights grew steadily colder. On November 24, near present-day Pueblo, Colorado, with the blue mountain seemingly no closer than when he had first seen it, Pike decided to stop and make a permanent camp.

Trees were felled, and a 5-foot-high (1.5-meter), three-sided breastwork was cobbled together. A breastwork is a hastily built military fortification usually chest high. When it was finished, Pike, Dr. Robinson, and Privates Miller and Brown set out northward in the direction of the towering mountain. Pike intended to climb it, thinking that from the top of the peak he would be able to map the surrounding area more easily. He estimated that it would be reachable within a few days' time. No one on the expedition was experienced in plains travel, nor did they realize how difficult it was to judge distance in the clear, dry air of the Southwest.

The men soon discovered that before they could get closer to the alluring blue peak they first had to cross another range, now called the Cheyenne Mountains, which ran parallel to the base of the distant mountain. Three days later, at the foot of a peak among the Cheyennes, they impulsively left their baggage and provisions behind and began an upward climb, confident that they could reach the top in a few hours. Instead darkness overtook them, the temperature fell to zero, and they took shelter in a cave "without blankets, victuals [food] or water."

On the morning of November 27—Thanksgiving Day, 1806—the men woke "hungry . . . and extremely sore from the inequality of the rocks on which we had lain all night." A heavy snow had fallen while they slept, but the sight that Pike beheld almost made the ordeal worth it. "The unbounded prairie was overhung with clouds, which appeared like an ocean in a storm; wave piled on wave and foaming, whilst the sky was perfectly clear where we were."

They resumed their upward march through a blanket of snow 3 feet (0.9 meter) deep surrounded by an eerie stillness, for there was "no sign of beast or bird inhabiting this region." An hour later, from

Pike believed the Rocky Mountains marked the boundary between the Louisiana Purchase and New Mexico. In the wide, open spaces of the West, it was hard for the explorer to judge distances. Mountains that seemed close at hand were actually miles off.

the top of a mountain, Pike could see that his goal, the even-taller peak—14,110 feet (4,304 meters) above sea level—was still several miles away. At that point, it would have been suicidal to proceed. Neither Pike nor his men had had anything to eat for two days; they were dressed only in "light overalls . . . and no stockings." The only sensible choice was to turn back.

Pike led his men down a deep ravine along what is now called Turkey Creek and found the baggage where they had left it. The food supply had been raided by wild animals, and only a few scraps remained. The four starving men found shelter under an outcropping of rock, then made a meal out of "a single partridge, and a piece of deer's ribs." On November 29, they finally arrived back at the stockade in the midst of a raging snowstorm.

PIKE NEVER CLIMBED
HIS PEAK

Pike called the mountain he had discovered on Thanksgiving Day, 1806, the Grand Peak, and concluded that "no human being could have ascended to its pinical [sic]." It was ascended, however, in the summer of 1820, by Dr. Edwin James and two other members of Major Stephen H. Long's Rocky Mountain expedition. When John C. Frémont explored the Rockies in 1843–1844, he called the mountain Pike's Peak, even though Zebulon Pike himself had never called it by that name, nor had he ever stood at its top. Pike was the first American to record having seen it, however, and the name Frémont gave it stuck—rightfully so.

Major Stephen H. Long headed a government expedition to the Rocky Mountains in 1820. Three members of Long's group were the first Americans to climb what was later named Pike's Peak, in honor of its discoverer.

By December 1, 1806, Pike's remaining horses were so sickly that hungry magpies boldly attacked them, "attracted by the scent of their sore backs." Nevertheless Pike pushed doggedly onward, hoping to do three things: to pick up the trail of the Spaniards, to find the source of the Arkansas River, then to locate the Red River. The following day, when they forded a river, two of the men "got their feet froze before we could get accommodated with a fire." On December 10, the starving horses were fed the only thing Pike had: "as there was nothing else for the latter to eat, gave them one pint of corn each."

For the men, there were no blankets for warmth; they had long since been cut into strips to be wrapped around the men's feet in place of socks that had worn out. The only way to keep warm at night was for the men to build huge fires—which meant expending precious energy to collect firewood—then huddle as close to the flames as possible, so "one side burned while the other was pierced by cold winds."

On Christmas Day, 1806, Pike let his men rest, but by January 5, 1807, he was forced to admit that what he'd hoped was the Red River was actually an outlet of the Arkansas, which he'd left a month earlier. The truth was, he was lost—and had been traveling in a large circle. It was a dispiriting moment, and he lamented, "This was my [twenty-eighth] birthday, and most fervently did I hope never to pass another so miserably."

Only a few horses were left, but they were too weak to be of any use. Sleds had to be built to transport food and baggage, and they had to be pulled by the men themselves, who were hardly any more capable than the horses. After leaving Antoine Vasquez and Patrick Smith behind with the horses and a few supplies, Pike headed south and once again ran into a forbidding chain of mountains that stretched across what are now the states of Colorado and New Mexico. Named the Sangre de Cristo (Blood of Christ) Mountains by the Spaniards, they were covered with snow and ice. Pike had learned a lesson. He knew better than to tackle them when confronted with the same obstacles that he had faced in the Rockies: lack of food and freezing temperatures. By this time, nine members of the expedition were suffering from badly frostbitten hands and feet, their fingers and toes so swollen that the skin began to split like the casings on roasted sausages.

On January 22, 1807, two more men—John Sparks and Thomas Daugherty—were left behind because their feet were so frostbitten it was impossible for them to walk. Sparks, of whom Pike was especially fond, had been an able hunter on the earlier journey up the Mississippi. Pike gave the two men his heartfelt assurance that he would send relief as soon as possible, and when he parted from them it was "not without tears."

The majestic peaks of the Rockies were often shrouded in mist, as depicted in this 1860s painting by Albert Bierstadt. It was such a peak that captured the imagination of Zebulon Pike and nearly cost him his life.

Five days later, on January 27, Henry Menaugh was also left behind. Conditions were almost more than a human being could bear, and Pike confessed in his journal, "for the first time in the voyage found myself discouraged." It is a testament to Pike's tenacity that he persevered; most men would have given up long before.

On the last day of January 1807, Pike halted the expedition and built a 36-square-foot (3.3-square-meter) stockade along what he believed was, at long last, the elusive Red River. He was mistaken. The headwaters of the Red River rise in the Texas Panhandle, far south of where he was camped. Around the inside walls of the fort, a ditch was dug and tall, sharp wooden stakes were driven into it, slanted toward the walls, to make it harder for an enemy to enter it by force. Was it Indians that they needed to be defended against? Or, as historians such as W. Eugene Hollon have suggested, did Pike know full well that he was deep in foreign territory and might need to defend himself against the Spanish?

On February 7, Dr. Robinson set out alone in the direction of what he hoped was Santa Fe. Pike had high regard for the young doctor, noting that he had been a fine "companion in danger, difficulties and hardship." On February 16, 1807, a Spanish cavalryman, accompanied by a single Indian companion, arrived at the stockade. They announced that Dr. Robinson had indeed reached Santa Fe alive and that help was on the way. Two days later, Sergeant William Meek and Private Theodore Miller volunteered to backtrack 200 miles (322 kilometers) to rescue Sparks and Daugherty. The two men were found alive, but because their feet were so severely damaged by frostbite, they both were destined "to be invalids for life . . . doomed to pass the remainder of their days in misery and want."

Ten days later, on February 26, 1807, one hundred Spanish soldiers under the command of two lieutenants, Bartholemew Fernandez and Ignatio Saltelo, arrived at Pike's stockade. They pointed out that Pike was in Spanish territory, that the river he had believed was the Red was

Was Pike Really Lost?

Historians have debated for almost two hundred years about whether or not Pike was actually lost. General Wilkinson wanted information about Spanish plans and activities in the region, and the best way to get it was to send someone to Santa Fe. Considering the tense relations between the United States and Spain, however, such a visit would not have been welcomed. But if an explorer—apparently not intending to do any mischief—were simply to wander accidentally into Spanish territory with a small group of men, it would be difficult to accuse him of deliberate wrongdoing. Pike could appear to have made an innocent mistake while still getting Wilkinson the information he wanted. The argument seems persuasive and would make Pike complicit in Wilkinson's scheme. But would Zebulon Pike have exposed himself and his men to such cruel physical conditions and life-threatening experiences to satisfy a mentor, even a mentor such as Wilkinson? It doesn't seem likely.

actually the Rio Grande. They offered to supply the Americans with horses, food, clothing, and whatever else they needed to get to the Red River. But first they had to report to Joaquin del Real Alencaster, the Spanish territorial governor in Santa Fe.

SIX

Prisoners — or Guests?

I immediately lowered my flag . . . and was conscious they must have positive orders to take me in.

—*Zebulon Pike, February 26, 1807*

Pike was hardly in a position to refuse the polite request of the Spanish officers to accompany them to Santa Fe—especially when an exchange with Lieutenant Fernandez made it clear that he and his men were camped on the banks of the Rio Grande.

"What [exclaimed Pike], is not this the Red river?"

"No sir! The Rio del Norte [Rio Grande]."

Pike hadn't forgotten Wilkinson's command not to cause alarm or offense to the Spanish. Fortunately Lieutenant Fernandez's gentlemanly manner made it easy to cooperate. "His mildness induced me to tell him that I would march," Pike said. Nevertheless it must have dawned on Pike that the request was in fact an order and that he and his men had been taken prisoner. On February 27, 1807, leaving two of his expedition members behind at the stockade in the company of fifty Spanish soldiers, Pike and his remaining five men—mounted on fresh horses, for the Spanish had specifically arrived with extra ones—were escorted southward.

After only three days of travel, the climate changed dramatically. It was "astonishing . . . we found ourselves on the plains where there was no snow, and where vegetation was sprouting." To heighten the

In 1807 Pike and his men were taken into custody by Spanish soldiers and escorted to Santa Fe. After the bitter wind and snow of the Rockies, the New Mexican landscape was a welcome, but stark, contrast.

contrast between the wretched suffering he and his men had recently endured in the snows of the mountains, in Agua Caliente (Warm Springs), a village of narrow streets populated by about five hundred "civilized Indians [of] much mixed blood," Pike observed the residents dancing a spirited fandango. The Spaniards told him they admired it so much they had introduced the dance to the royal court in Madrid.

On March 2, 1807, the entourage arrived in San Juan (Saint John's), a village of about one thousand that was entirely enclosed by a mud wall. Women from the village came to tend to the damaged feet of Pike's men, and everyone was given something to eat. As the Americans were about to enter lodgings that had been provided for them, Baptiste La Lande, a French trader, approached Pike and whispered in broken English. "I am very sorry to see you here: we are all prisoners in this country. I have been here three years and cannot get out." If Pike was concerned about his own fate, he put a brave face on it. He informed La Lande tersely that "with respect to myself, I [feel] no apprehension."

Although Pike claimed to have no apprehension about his fate at the hands of the Spaniards, he probably had a few twinges once he got to Santa Fe, where he was greeted in a hostile manner by Governor Alencaster. "Do you speak French?" the governor demanded coldly. All around the world, French was the language of educated men, and Pike prided himself that he did, indeed, speak it. As a result, the two men were able to talk without an interpreter.

The governor accused Pike of intending to spy on the Spanish. Pike energetically denied the charge. He explained that his only intention had been to explore the territory recently acquired by his own country, a territory whose boundaries hadn't yet been clearly mapped. The governor demanded to see Pike's military orders, which General Wilkinson had been careful to word in such a way that no ulterior motives could be inferred by the Spanish in case Pike was apprehended. Then, after examining the contents of

MYSTERIOUS MOTIVES

Pike called Dr. Robinson "the right arm of the expedition" and admired the young man's steady aim when they hunted together. He might have been surprised to learn that Robinson hoped to collect a debt from none other than Baptiste La Lande, the Frenchman who confided to Pike that he had been the Spaniards' prisoner for three years. Pike would have been even more startled had he known that Robinson told Spanish officials he wished to become a Spanish citizen, convert to the Catholic faith, and requested that Pike not be informed of his intentions. Robinson even offered to become an explorer on behalf of the Spanish. Officials were suspicious of the doctor's true motives, and he was later returned to the United States.

Pike's trunk, Alencaster told him that he must go to Chihuahua in present-day Mexico to appear before Commander General Nemesio Salcedo.

Pike wondered aloud, "If we go . . . must [we] be considered prisoners of war?" Alencaster, who by this time had begun to warm to Pike, was quick to reassure him. "By no means," he soothed. "I know you do not go voluntarily, but I will give you a certificate . . . of my having obliged you to march," in the event Pike was later questioned by his

The Spanish were surprised at the ragged appearance of the Americans. The condition of his and his men's clothes embarrassed Pike, a man who was always eager to make a good impression.

own superiors. The words were enough to set Pike's mind at ease and to allow him to enjoy the hospitality offered by the Spanish.

"During dinner, at which we had a variety of wines, [we] were entertained with music, composed of bass drums, French horns, violins and cymbals." On that occasion, perhaps Pike foreswore his abstinence from alcohol.

Pike and his men, along with Dr. Robinson, were escorted to Chihuahua by Lieutenant Melgares, the same Spanish officer whose trail Pike had been so eager to locate as he crossed the prairie. On April 2, Spanish officials questioned Pike closely, his papers were inspected again, and twenty-one of them were removed from his trunk.

Salcedo wasn't as overtly hostile as Governor Alencaster had been. Nevertheless he was convinced that Pike was a spy who had deliberately intruded on Spanish territory. As a result, the Spanish ambassador in Washington, D.C., was instructed to make a formal protest to President Jefferson, who by this time was fully acquainted with the details of Pike's expedition. Jefferson defended Pike, explaining that he'd simply lost his way in a country that Americans knew little about and that he hadn't intended to commit any crime against Spanish sovereignty.

Throughout their stay in Chihuahua, Pike and his men were well treated. Their food, lodging, and personal needs were tended to with courtesy. Finally, after further conversations with Pike, Governor Salcedo concluded that Pike ought to be released and sent back to the United States. However, for reasons that were never made clear, five of Pike's men were detained for two years before they were allowed to return. On April 28, 1807, Melgares escorted Pike and the men who had been freed out of the city. Before they parted, Melgares warned Pike that he "should not be permitted to make any astronomical observations"—to read the stars—for the purpose of mapping, to which Pike replied that he was well aware he was on Spanish territory and would not do so. That didn't mean, however, that he didn't take careful note of Spanish forts, their locations, and the number of soldiers stationed at each. He had not forgotten that his country and Spain were enemies, nor that war between them was looming.

Several months later, on July 1, 1807, Pike arrived in Natchitoches, Louisiana Territory. He'd been gone almost a year and returned not to a glorious reception, but to the unfolding of yet another scandal that whirled around General Wilkinson. Aaron Burr, the general's old crony, had been arrested for treason. Wilkinson, realizing Burr's scheme was unraveling fast, had alerted President Jefferson to the plot to invade Mexico, conveniently denying his own involvement in it. True to his old habit of turning against a friend to save his own reputation, he had offered to be the government's main witness against Burr.

PACIFIC

OCEAN

ROCKY MOUNTAINS

Missouri River

Leech
Lake

SPANISH

POSSESSIONS

INDIANA
TERRITORY

▲ Pike's Peak
• Pueblo

St. Louis •

KENTUCKY

• Santa Fe

Arkansas River

Mississippi River

TENNESSEE

Red River

MISSISSIPPI

TERRITORY

Natchitoches •

Rio Grande

Chihuahua •

MEXICO

1805–1806 ——
1806–1807 ——
Louisiana Purchase ------

ZEBULON PIKE'S ROUTES

The charge against Burr was supported by a great deal of evidence against him, which the government had collected. One unexpected result of the investigation, however, was that for the first time it became public knowledge that Wilkinson had for many years been a paid informant of the Spanish government. In spite of his efforts to save himself, Wilkinson was caught in the same net that swept up Burr. The government's case was strong, and it was assumed that the trial would be swift and the penalties harsh. To the amazement of many, both Burr and Wilkinson were acquitted of all charges. Burr fled to Europe, while Wilkinson faced an investigation of other matters and a potential court-martial.

Pike was no doubt astonished that, because of his close association with Wilkinson, he was under suspicion as well. Once again, rather than being given a reception like the one Lewis and Clark had received, Pike discovered that his reputation—not to mention his entire mission to the Southwest—was being called into question. The public, stimulated by newspaper articles, demanded to know if Pike was a spy, as the Spanish had claimed. How much did he know about Wilkinson and Burr's plans? Had the general given him secret orders? If so, what were they?

Critics pointed out that the Lewis and Clark expedition had been sanctioned by Jefferson himself. Pike's mission to the Southwest, on the other hand, like the one up the Mississippi, had been at the behest of Wilkinson, not the president. As a result, Pike found himself treated coldly by his superiors. His fellow officers were uncomfortable in his presence as well, and whispers of suspicion continually dogged him.

Pike, ever anxious to be admired, was bitter and humiliated. He wrote to Henry Dearborn, the U.S. secretary of war, seeking to have his name cleared. Dearborn replied, "You may rest assured that your services are held in high estimation by the President . . . and . . . I can very frankly declare that I consider the public much indebted to you." The words were reassuring, but the public—fueled by various newspapers' implications of wrongdoing—continued to regard him as a controversial figure.

In September 1807, after some much-deserved rest, Pike, Clara, and their four-year-old daughter (also named Clara, the only one of their children to live to adulthood) moved to Washington, D.C., where he hoped to organize his papers and prepare them for publication. Pike had a chance to meet personally with Dearborn and on two occasions

(13)

who returned the compliment (on the 10ᵗʰ
of Aug.) by killing 10 Sioux at the entrance
of the St. Peters. Also that a war party composed
of the Sacks, Reynards and Puants of 200
Warriors had embarked on an expidition
against the Sauteaux — but that they had
heard that the Chief having had an unfa-
-vourable dream persuaded the Party to
return. and that I would meet them on my
voyage.

Here I was introduced to a Chief
called the Raven of the Reynards — he made
a very flowery speech on the occasion; which I
returned — in a few words, accompanied by
a small present.

It was about embarking
and giveing my two men over for lost when
a pirogue arrived in which was a Mr. Blondeau,
two Frenchmen, and my two men; whom the above
named Gentleman had engaged at the
little Town above the Rapids of Stony
River: They had been six days without
any thing to eate except muscles — when they
met Mr. Faribault Read whose humanity,
and attention to them; partly restored their
strength, and spirits, and enabled them
to reach the Reynard Village where they met
Mr. Blondeau. The Indian Chief furnished
them with Corn and shoes and shewo his
friendship by every possible attention.
I immediately discharge the hire of the Indians
and give Mr. Blondeau a passage into the
Prairie Des Chiens. Leave the Lead mines
at past 4 of. Distance. 25 miles

A page from the journal kept by Zebulon Pike during his southwestern
explorations. A mostly self-educated man, Pike was particularly proud
of his abilities as a writer, chronicling his adventures along the frontier.

After Pike's journals were published in 1810, American traders began traveling into New Mexico. Despite the objections of Spanish authorities, these traders used what would became a well-traveled route known as the Santa Fe Trail.

met with Jefferson himself, receiving from each man additional assurance that his contribution to the growing knowledge of the Southwest was appreciated. Jefferson signaled this attitude by giving Pike permission to publish the journals he'd kept of his Mississippi explorations of 1805–1806, as well as of his recent foray into Lower Louisiana.

In 1810 the journals were published in Philadelphia by C. & A. Conrad & Company and printed by Joseph Binns, who had been the first to print the U.S. Constitution. *An Account of Expeditions to the Sources of the Mississippi, and Through the Western Parts of Louisiana* placed Pike on the brink of the sort of fame he'd always dreamed of. Pike's journal sparked the interest of American traders in Saint Louis who soon made their way to Santa Fe despite the objections of the Spanish authorities.

Once a commercial link was established, American domination of trade and politics in the region was only a matter of time. On July 18, 1811, the Washington *National Intelligencer* favorably concluded that Pike "well merits the thanks of his countrymen." In 1811 the journals were also published in England, then in France, Germany, and Holland, where they caused an increase in emigration to the United States from those nations.

As Pike was working on his journals, talk of war whirled through the capital. But the anticipated conflict was not with Spain, as had been expected, but with Britain. Pike was eager to serve in whatever capacity he could and asked for a new command. The request was turned down, but a short time later he was commissioned a major in the Sixth Infantry. He was also able to get his brother George, then fifteen years old, admitted to West Point, which meant a great deal to the explorer. He had stern advice to give young George, though, while at the same time giving himself a needed pat on the back.

"[L]et your arms [weapons] be your best—your clothes appropriate to your rank—and your behavior such as is becoming [to] . . . the brother of a man not unknown to the army." Pike was fifteen years old himself when he'd entered the military and had earned his rank the rough-and-tumble way, without the benefit of the kind of training George would get at West Point. Not that Pike had any regrets about the career he'd chosen. He would never think of himself as anything other than a soldier, and he still longed to distinguish himself in a way that would continue to lift him far above his peers.

S E V E N

fame or Death

*I embark tomorrow [from] Sackett's harbor. . . . If success attends
my steps, honor and glory await my name.*
                    —*Zebulon Pike's last letter to his father, April 1813*

Pike returned to New Orleans in January 1809, amid increased talk of a
second war with Britain. For the next three years he held various commands
throughout the South, becoming a lieutenant colonel in the process.

The United States became increasingly fearful that the British
might try to capture or blockade New Orleans, a bustling port city of
25,000 at the mouth of the Mississippi. New Orleans was the center of
trade in homegrown cotton, livestock, and agricultural products as well
as imported goods from many nations. Its loss would cause serious
hardship to the fledgling American economy. Therefore preparations

When Pike returned from the Southwest, he was assigned the task of draining the swamps along the lower Mississippi River. Then fortifications were built to guard against possible British invasion.

were under way to defend New Orleans if war came to pass. On May 29, 1809, Pike received orders to establish a cantonment, a temporary base for supplying and training troops, at *Terre aux Boeufs* (Land of the Oxen), 12 miles (19 kilometers) south of the city.

WHY BATTLE THE BRITISH TWICE?

The War of 1812 was, in a sense, a continuation of the conflict with the British that hadn't been resolved by the Revolutionary War. Although the American colonies had won their freedom, they still depended on European nations, including Britain, for many manufactured goods. In 1803, when war broke out between France and England, Britain tightened its control over all seagoing commerce, which meant that European countries were prevented from trading freely with the United States. The British reconsidered their embargo after an American frigate, the *President*, ordered to protect U.S. trade, defeated Britain's *Little Belt* in May 1811. But U.S. officials were in no mood to negotiate with the British on the issue of restricted trade. Leaders in Washington, D.C., were also angered by the fact that England continued to supply weapons to Indian tribes from its Canadian provinces, weapons that were used against American settlers in the western colonies. Americans were also aggravated by the act of "impressment." The British routinely boarded American merchant ships to search for deserters from the British Navy. When found, the men were removed by force and pressed back into service on British vessels, where their pay and treatment were poor. Americans came to believe that a second war with the British—a war that would decisively drive them out of Canada—seemed not only inevitable but desirable.

The cold and snow of the Rocky Mountains during the winter had been terrible; the heat, humidity, and mosquitoes of New Orleans during the summer were almost worse. Throughout the summer of 1809, Pike, with 3,000 men under his command, struggled against the demoralizing effects of malaria, food that rotted quickly in the damp climate, and the lack of medical supplies. Meanwhile the soldiers continued to labor, draining swamps and building levees. Sometimes Pike himself was the only one healthy enough to tend the sick or to bury them when they didn't recover.

Pike's commanding officer at the time, the man who had selected the site for such endeavors, was none other than General James Wilkinson, who seemed able to emerge from any scandal unscathed. His orders from the war department had been to select higher ground *north* of the city, not south. But Wilkinson, who couldn't resist a chance for personal gain, had secretly arranged with Jean Delassize, owner of the swamp, not only to build the cantonment there but in the process to convert the property into land suitable for planting sugarcane. In return Wilkinson expected to share in whatever profits were made on Delassize's crops.

After several hundred men died of malaria at the cantonment, the government ordered Wilkinson to abandon the site. A congressional investigation examined Pike's role in the matter and cleared him of wrongdoing, but the press—which had willingly piled blame on Pike for the debacle in Santa Fe—was less charitable. On September 16, 1809, an article in the Natchez *Weekly Chronicle* described Pike as "a soldier of yesterday, a parasite of Wilkinson."

Such criticism came at a time when Pike had plenty of other worries. His wife was pregnant with their fifth child (the baby, a boy, died not long after his birth). His brother James had arrived in New Orleans and was seriously ill with tuberculosis. His younger brother, George, for whom Pike had arranged an appointment to West Point, had written to the secretary of war requesting five months' pay in advance, a reckless breach of military conduct.

CHAMPION OF SECOND CHANCES

If General James Wilkinson had created such inexcusable mischief for so many years, why was he granted numerous second chances? The answer is that the newly formed United States didn't have a large standing army. In 1808, for example, the nation's population was only 7 million, and the army had only 6,744 regulars in two infantry regiments, one artillery regiment, and one corps of engineers. Nor did the army have many qualified officers. Wilkinson, using his charm and the silver tongue for which he was famous, discounted his past mistakes and pointed to his years of service as a way of wrangling new positions. And he usually got what he asked for. As soon as he did, he reverted to what he did best: working for personal gain.

"Have you lost your senses—do you know that your letter will be treated with contempt?" Pike scolded. He couldn't have known that conditions at the academy were at a low point. A mere fifteen cadets were enrolled, taught by only two instructors. Nor would Pike have been so vexed had he known that George was far more ill than James and didn't have long to live. As if such concerns weren't heavy enough, Pike's mother died on Christmas Day, 1809.

Meanwhile Wilkinson's continued misconduct finally resulted in his removal from his post. General Wade Hampton, who replaced him, dismissed Pike as well. The Natchez *Weekly Chronicle* was delighted and wrote on March 5, 1810, "We learn[ed] with great pleasure" that Pike would be removed. The newspaper went on to ridicule him as "the knight of Santa Fe." Wilkinson was brought before a military court in Washington, D.C., to face several charges, including graft and waste of public funds. Amazingly he was acquitted once again!

By 1812 rumors of war with Britain entered the realm of fact. A declaration of war, urged by the "war hawks" in Washington, D.C.,—including Henry Clay of Kentucky and John C. Calhoun of South Carolina, who represented states that were suffering the consequences of Britain's supplying weapons to the Indians—was pushed through the U.S. House of Representatives and Senate. War was declared on June 18, and soon after, on July 6, Pike was promoted to full colonel. When he received his orders to go to the front, he wrote to his father, "You will hear either of my fame or my death."

In late July, Pike received orders to add new recruits to his regiment, the Fifteenth. The men had to be "free from sore legs, scurvy, scalded [scabby] heads, ruptures, and other infirmities." Boys between fourteen and eighteen years of age were accepted with their parents' permission. A month later the regiment was six to seven hundred strong, although many of the recruits had never fired a rifle in their lives and had no sense of military discipline. But even Pike's critics gave him credit for his unique ability: he knew how to turn raw recruits into soldiers the country could be proud of.

While Pike gathered his regiment, the first attempt was made by American troops to invade Canada. The outcome was dismal, for on August 16, 1812, General William Hull surrendered Detroit, on the border between the two countries, without firing a single shot. Then a second humiliating defeat befell American troops in October at Queenston Heights on the Niagara River in New York. Nevertheless preparations continued for a main offensive against Montreal under

General Henry Dearborn (1751-1859), former U.S. secretary of war, directed the offensive against the British at Montreal. One of the officers in his command was Colonel Zebulon Pike.

the leadership of General Dearborn, the former secretary of war. Under his command were General Joseph Bloomfield, General John Chandler, and Colonel Zebulon Pike.

On November 16, the army began its march toward Canada, reaching Champlain, 20 miles (32 kilometers) north of Plattsburgh, New York, near the southern boundary of the province of Quebec. On November 21, Pike and his troops encountered a small force of British soldiers along with their Indian allies and routed them easily. Pike burned the enemy's encampment and was prepared to press on when, to his great dismay, Dearborn ordered a retreat to Plattsburgh. With winter coming on, any further invasion had to be put off until spring.

On April 5, 1813, Pike was notified of his promotion to general and later that month, as the ice began to melt in Sacketts Harbor (now spelled *Sackets*) on Lake Ontario, the invasion of York (present-day Toronto) began. After crossing the lake aboard the *Madison*, Pike and his troops overran a British force that had been sent there to meet them. General R. H. Sheaffe realized that continued resistance against the American onslaught would be futile and raised a white flag. Pike had spent his life in the army, but this was his first victory on a battlefield. With considerable satisfaction, he ordered one of his men forward to discuss terms of a formal surrender with the British commander.

Suddenly a tremendous explosion shattered the air. Some of the retreating British soldiers had fired into one of their own magazines—a storehouse for gunpowder—only a few yards from where Pike stood. It blew up, hurling wood, rocks, and debris through the air for hundreds of yards. Fifty-two men were killed, among them Captain Joseph Nicholson, Pike's military aide, and 180 were wounded. Forty-two British soldiers were killed as well. One of the rocks, propelled with the force of a cannonball, struck Pike in the back, crushing his spine and ribs and leaving a gaping, bloody hole.

Pike, thirty-four years old, realized he couldn't survive such a massive injury. "I am mortally wounded—my ribs and back are stove in," he said. "Push on . . . and avenge your general," he urged, as he was carried aboard the *Madison*, which waited along shore. When the British flag was taken down a few hours later, it was delivered to Pike. He asked to have it folded and placed beneath his head. He died a few minutes later. One story has it that because there was no other way to preserve Pike's body before burial, it was placed in a hogshead, or barrel, of whiskey.

On the night before his death, Pike had written to Clara, remarking that it was only natural to wish "to communicate with those we love, more especially when we conceive it may be the last time in this world. Should I fail, defend my memory [and] remember me with a father's love . . . to our daughter." It was as if he had a presentiment of impending doom.

Pike's grave site in the cemetery near Fort Tompkins was marked by a simple wooden slab. In 1819 his body was removed to an official

On April 27, 1813, Zebulon Pike—having earned a general's commission only three weeks earlier—was mortally wounded at York (present-day Toronto) when an ammunition storehouse exploded.

The capture of the British barracks at York, begun under Pike's command, was considered the first American victory of the War of 1812. Unfortunately Pike did not live long enough to savor the victory or the elusive fame he had always pursued.

burial site at the fort, along with the bodies of others who had died in the explosion. After a time the graves, left untended, became overgrown with weeds, and it was difficult to tell who was buried where. In 1909, almost a century later, the entire graveyard was moved again to a site not far from Sacketts Harbor, where a small granite headstone now marks Zebulon Pike's final resting place. For many years, officials in Colorado sought unsuccessfully to have Pike reburied near the peak that bears his name.

The fame that had eluded Pike during his lifetime found him at last in death. The Battle of York was considered to be the first American victory in the War of 1812, and a special tribute was paid to Pike by President James Madison in a speech before Congress. A newly completed warship in Sacketts Harbor was christened the *General Pike*, and on

September 28, 1812, it defeated a British warship on Lake Ontario. Pike became a national hero—precisely what he'd always longed to be.

After Pike's death, General Wilkinson's seemingly endless store of luck finally ran out. His political clout in Washington, D.C., diminished after the end of the War of 1812, and he was no longer able to wrangle favors as he'd done in the past. He went to Mexico and applied for a land grant as payment for his past service to the Spanish government. His request was flatly refused. He then became addicted to opium and died on December 28, 1825.

The mysterious Dr. Robinson returned to Mexico as a spy acting on behalf of the U.S. government. The Spanish weren't deceived, however, and sent him right back where he came from. Robinson then called for adventurous Americans to join him in liberating the Mexican masses from Spanish rule and became a general in the revolutionary forces that existed within Mexico. When a planned uprising didn't take place as he'd hoped, Robinson returned to New Orleans, where he died in September 1819, six years after Pike's death at York.

Today many counties, cities, small towns, lakes, and rivers across America are named Pike, though not because of the young general's battlefield death in the final war against England. Instead Zebulon Montgomery Pike is remembered best for having been the first American to gaze upon a tall peak in the Colorado Rockies that he somewhat whimsically called "a small blue cloud" when he first saw it. It is a mountain that, ironically, he never named and never climbed.

ZEBULON PIKE
AND HIS TIMES

1776 The Declaration of Independence is adopted on July 4 by the thirteen American colonies.

1779 Zebulon Montgomery Pike is born on January 5 near present-day Trenton, New Jersey.

1781 The American Revolution comes to an end.

1792 Pike's father moves the family to Fort Washington, Ohio, where fourteen-year-old Zeb meets General James Wilkinson.

1793 Pike enlists in the army.

1799 Pike becomes a second lieutenant under Wilkinson's command. Eight months later, he is promoted to full lieutenant.

1801 Pike marries his cousin Clarissa "Clara" Brown.

1803 The U.S. government buys the Louisiana Territory from France for $15 million.

1804 Meriwether Lewis and William Clark begin their journey—called the Corps of Discovery—to explore the newly acquired region.

1805 General Wilkinson sends Pike up the Mississippi River on the pretext of locating its headwaters.

1806 In July Pike begins a southwestern expedition at General Wilkinson's request. On Thanksgiving Day, Pike sees what he describes as "a small blue cloud" and calls it the Grand Peak. He later becomes lost in the Rockies.

1807 In February Pike and his men are taken into custody in Spanish territory, accused of being spies, and released a few months later.

1812 War is declared against Britain. The United States invades Canada.

1813 On April 27, Pike dies at the age of thirty-four at the Battle of York near present-day Toronto.

1820 Pike's Peak is climbed for the first time by three members of Major Stephen H. Long's Rocky Mountain expedition.

Further Research

Books

Baker, Nina Brown. *Pike of Pike's Peak.* New York: Harcourt, Brace, 1988.

Keating, Bern. *Zebulon Pike.* New York: G.P. Putnam's Sons, 1965.

Sinnott, Susan. *Zebulon Pike.* Chicago: Children's Press, 1990.

Stallones, Jared. *Zebulon Pike and the Explorers of the American Southwest.* New York: Chelsea House, 1992.

Wibberly, Leonard. *Zebulon Pike: Soldier and Explorer.* New York: Funk & Wagnalls, 1961.

Videos

The American Frontier. Schlessinger Media, P.O. Box 580, Wynnewood, PA 19096. Grades 5 to 8.

Web Sites

Westward Expansion–Zebulon Pike Links
http://www.foresthills.edu/maddux/gowest.html#Zebulon%20Pike

Zebulon Montgomery Pike
http://dlwgraphics.com/mnpike2.htm

Zebulon Montgomery Pike: American Explorer
http://www.enchantedlearning.com/explorers/page/p/pike.shtml

Zebulon Pike: Hard-Luck Explorer or Successful Spy?
http://www.nps.gov/jeff/LewisClark2/Circa1804/WestwardExpansion/ EarlyExplorers/ZebulonPike.htm

Bibliography

Coues, Elliot. *The Expeditions of Zebulon Montgomery Pike*, vol. 1. Minneapolis: Ross and Haines, Inc., 1965. (Reprinted in full from original 1810 edition)

Hollon, W. Eugene. *The Lost Pathfinder: Zebulon Montgomery Pike*. Norman, OK: University of Oklahoma Press, 1949.

Jackson, Donald. "How Lost Was Zebulon Pike?" *Journal of American Heritage*, vol. 16, February 1965, pp. 10–15, 75–80.

———. *The Journals of Zebulon Montgomery Pike: With Letters and Related Documents*, vols. 1 and 2. Norman, OK: University of Oklahoma Press, 1966.

Milner, Clyde A., II, Carol A. O'Connor, and Martha A. Sandweiss, eds. *The Oxford History of the American West*. New York: Oxford University Press, 1994.

Ruth, Kent. *Great Day in the West: Forts, Posts, and Rendezvous Beyond the Mississippi*. Norman, OK: University of Oklahoma Press, 1963.

Sanford, William R. *Zebulon Pike: Explorer of the Southwest*. Springfield, NJ: Enslow Publishers, Inc., 1996.

Terrell, John Upton. *Zebulon Pike: The Life and Times of an Adventurer*. New York: Weybright and Talley, 1968.

Viola, Herman J. *Exploring the West*. Washington, D.C.: Smithsonian Books, 1987.

Wyckoff, William, and Lary M. Dilsaver, eds. *The Mountainous West: Explorations in Historical Geography*. Lincoln: University of Nebraska Press, 1995.

Source Notes

Foreword:

p. 4: "an admirable trumpeter": Donald Jackson, *The Journals of Zebulon Montgomery Pike: With Letters and Related Documents*, vol 2 (University of Oklahoma Press, 1966), p. 102.

p. 5: "a knave . . . from petty chicanery": Jackson, p. 102.

Chapter One:

p. 6: "No officer could be": Jared Stallones, *Zebulon Pike and the Explorers of the American Southwest* (Chelsea House, 1992), p. 31.

p. 7: "Our second child Zebulon was born": W. Eugene Hollon, *The Lost Pathfinder: Zebulon Montgomery Pike* (University of Oklahoma Press, 1949), p. 8.

p. 7: "boy of slender form . . . the child was father to the man": Hollon, p. 10.

p. 10: "slight in quality": Elliott Coues, *The Expeditions of Zebulon Montgomery Pike*, (Ross and Haines, Inc., 1965), vol. 1, p. xxi.

p. 10: "badly clothed, badly fed, and badly paid": John Upton Terrell, *Zebulon Pike: The Life and Times of an Adventurer* (Weybright and Talley, 1968), p. 29.

p. 10: "I cannot live . . .": Hollon, p. 14.

p. 11: "unprincipled imbecile . . . rascal through and through . . . a rare faculty for": Coues, p. lv.

p. 11: "a handsome, charming, silver-tongued": Stallones, p. 19.

p. 14: "you will hear either of my fame or my death": Stallones, p. 30.

p. 14: "Tolerably square and robust": William R. Sanford, *Zebulon Pike: Explorer of the Southwest* (Enslow, 1996), p. 14.

p. 16: "the most vexatious evil": Coues, p. xxiv.

p. 16: "tolerably handsome": Hollon, p. 24.

p. 17: "youth is subject to errors. . . . Whilst I have . . . breath": Hollon, p. 27.

Chapter Two:

p. 18: "proceed up the Mississippi": Donald Jackson, *The Journals of Zebulon Montgomery Pike: With Letters and Related Documents*, (University of Oklahoma Press, 1966), vol. 1, p. 3.

p. 18: "a mean looking village": Sanford, p. 14.

p. 18: "The French residents were lazy": Bern Keating, *Zebulon Pike* (G. P. Putnam's Sons, 1965), p. 17.

p. 19: "Nothing is to be seen but houses": Keating, p. 18.

p. 23: "ascend the main branches of the River": Jackson, p. 3.

p. 23: "knew what he was to do": Terrell, p. 43.

p. 24: "flour, cornmeal, pork": Keating, p. 21.

p. 24: "[we] were so unfortunate": Coues, p. 7.

p. 24: "our boat struck a sawyer . . . we with great difficulty": Coues, p. 12.

p. 25: "with several successive ridges": Coues, p. 14.

p. 26: "thanked me for the good opinion": Coues, p. 17.

p. 26: "boat never waited for any person": Coues, p. 21.

p. 26: "all strangers are enemies": Jackson, p. 16.

p. 27: "six days without . . . humanity and attention": Coues, p. 32.

p. 29: "the finest site on the Mississippi": Coues, p. 82.

p. 29: "a much better soldier than": Hollon, p. 69.

p. 29: "three geese, and one raccoon": Coues, p. 95.

p. 29: "one of the stoutest men I ever knew . . . a pint of blood": Hollon, p. 71.

p. 29: "these unhappy circumstances": Coues, p. 105.

Chapter Three:

p. 30: "I began to conceive the life of a Hunter": Hollon, p. 59.

p. 30: "every hand to work": Coues, p. 107.

p. 32: "ice in the river": Coues, p. 113.

p. 32: "powerfully attacked with fantastics of the brain": Coues, p.121.

p. 35: "Gave out two pound[s] of extra meat": Jackson, p. 73.

p. 35: "Never did I undergo more fatigue": Hollon, p. 74.

p. 35: "At night I was scarcely able": Hollon, p. 74.

p. 35: "I will not attempt to describe my feeling": Jackson, p. 87.

p. 37: "They have horses": Hollon, p. 77.

p. 38: "considered it strictly my duty": Hollon, pp. 84–85.

p. 40: "All our great men": Hollon, p. 85.

Chapter Four:

p. 41: "[Y]ou are herewith furnished": Jackson, p. 287.

p. 44: "it will be necessary that you should move": Hollon, p. 101.

p. 44: "be held responsible . . . I refer you to your orders": Hollon, p. 102.

p. 45: "tempered by degrees. . . . Do not push him": Stallones, p. 57.

p. 47: "the Americans [who] stretched forth their hands": Leonard Wibberly, *Zebulon Pike: Soldier and Explorer* (Funk Wagnalls, 1961), p. 99.

p. 47: "large quantities of corn": Hollon, p. 107.

p. 47: "very unpleasant news": Hollon, p. 110.

p. 47: "These vast plains": Jackson, vol. 2, p. 27.

p. 48: "Every morning [as the sun comes up]": Hollon, p. 104.

p. 48: "tall, slim [with] high cheekbones . . . raising horses: Jackson, vol. 2, pp. 34–35.

p. 50: "the grand principle by which": Jackson, vol. 2, p. 37.

p. 52: "A smooth piece of ground": Jackson, vol. 2, p. 38.

Chapter Five:

p. 54: "We had great difficulty": Jackson, vol. 1, p. 363.

p. 54: "My men have no winter cloathing": Jackson, vol. 2, p. 161.

p. 55: "one of the most poorly equipped": Terrell, p. 135.

p. 55: "Our horses are very much jaded . . . entirely gave out": Jackson, vol. 1, p. 344.

p. 55: "a mountain . . . which looked like a small blue cloud": Jackson, vol. 1, p. 344.

p. 55: "natural boundary between": Jackson, vol. 1, p. 345.

p. 57: "without blankets, victuals or water": Jackson, vol. 1, p. 350.

p. 57: "hungry . . . and extremely sore": Jackson, vol. 1, p. 350.

p. 57: "The unbounded prairie": Jackson, vol. 1, p. 350.

p. 57: "no sign of beast or bird": Jackson, vol. 1, p. 350.

p. 58: "light overalls . . . and no stockings": Jackson, vol. 1, p. 351.

p. 58: "a single partridge": Jackson, vol. 1, p. 351.

p. 59: "no human being could have ascended": Hollon, p. 128.

p. 60: "attracted by the scent": Jackson, vol. 1, p. 353.

p. 60: "got their feet froze before we could": Jackson, vol. 1, p. 353.

p. 60: "as there was nothing else": Jackson, vol. 1, p. 356.

p. 60: "one side burned": Jackson, vol. 1, p. 356.

p. 60: "This was my [twenty-eighth] birthday": Jackson, vol. 1, p. 366.

p. 61: "not without tears": Jackson, vol. 1, p. 371.

p. 62: "for the first time in the voyage": Jackson, vol. 1, p. 371.

p. 62: "companion in danger": Hollon, p. 137.

p. 62: "to be invalids for life": Jackson, vol. 1, p. 381.

Chapter Six:

p. 64: "I immediately lowered my flag": Jackson, vol. 1, p. 384.

p. 64: "What [exclaimed Pike]": Jackson, vol. 1, p. 384.

p. 64: "His mildness induced me to tell him": Jackson, vol. 1, p. 384.

p. 65: "astonishing . . . we found ourselves": Jackson, vol. 1, p. 387.

p. 66: "civilized Indians": Jackson, vol. 1, p. 387.

p. 66: "I am very sorry to see you here": Jackson, vol. 1, p. 388.

p. 66: "with respect to myself": Jackson, vol. 1, p. 388.

p. 66: "Do you speak French?": Jackson, vol. 1, p. 392.

p. 67: "the right arm of the expedition": Donald Jackson, "How Lost Was Zebulon Pike?" *Journal of American Heritage*, (vol. 16, February 1965), p. 78.

p. 67: "If we go": Jackson, vol. 1, p. 394.

p. 67: "By no means": Jackson, vol. 1, p. 394.

p. 68: "During dinner, at which we had": Jackson, vol. 1, p. 399.

p. 69: "should not be permitted": Jackson, vol. 1, p. 423.

p. 71: "You may rest assured": Wibberly, p. 161.

p. 74: "well merits the thanks": Hollon, p. 178.

p. 74: "[L]et your arms [weapons] be your best": Hollon, p. 174.

Chapter Seven:

p. 75: "I embark tomorrow": Terrell, p. 233.

p. 78: "a soldier of yesterday": Hollon, p. 185.

p. 79: "Have you lost your senses": Hollon, p. 187.

p. 80: "We learn[ed] with great pleasure": Hollon, p. 188.

p. 80: "You will hear either of my fame or my death": Wibberly, p. 168.

p. 80: "free from sore legs": Hollon, p. 203.

p. 82: "I am mortally wounded": Hollon, p. 217.

p. 83: "to communicate with those we love": Hollon, p. 217.

p. 85: "a small blue cloud": Jackson, vol. 1, p. 344.

INDEX

Page numbers in **boldface** are illustrations.

Index